Editors
Karen Tam Froloff
Eric Migliaccio

Managing Editor
Ina Levin

Editor-in-Chief
Sharon Coan, M.S. Ed.

Cover Artist
Janet Chadwick

Art Manager
Kevin Barnes

Art Director
CJae Froshay

Imaging
Alfred Lau
James Edward Grace
Rosa C. See

Product Manager
Phil Garcia

Publisher
Mary D. Smith, M.S. Ed.

Grammar, Usage & Mechanics

GRADE 5

Author

Melissa Hart, M.F.A

Teacher Created Resources, Inc.
6421 Industry Way
Westminster, CA 92683
www.teachercreated.com
ISBN: 978-0-7439-3780-1
©2003 Teacher Created Resources, Inc.
Reprinted, 2008
Made in U.S.A.

Table of Contents

Introduction

The idea that "practice makes perfect" relates directly to your child's education. The more practice your child receives in concepts being taught in school, the more success he or she will achieve. Many parents know the value of practicing a subject learned in school, but the lack of readily available resources can be frustrating.

As a parent, it is also difficult to know where to focus your efforts so that the practice your child receives at home supports what he or she is being taught at school.

This book was written with the goal of helping both parents and teachers reinforce basic language skills with children. *Practice Makes Perfect: Grammar, Usage & Mechanics* reviews grammar skills for fifth grade students. The exercises in this book can be completed sequentially or out of order, as needed.

Completing this book will help your child meet the following fifth grade standards and objectives, which are similar to those required by your state and school district:

- The student uses nouns, pronouns, adjectives, adverbs, and coordinating conjunctions in written compositions.
- The student uses capitalization appropriately.
- The student avoids double negatives.
- The student uses question marks after interrogative sentences and exclamation marks after exclamatory sentences.
- The student uses apostrophes in contractions and possessive nouns.
- The student uses quotation marks around direct quotations.
- The student uses a colon between hours and minutes.
- The student uses strategies to organize written work.
- The student evaluates his or her own and others' writing.
- The student uses strategies to draft and revise written work.

How to Make the Most of This Book

Here are some ideas to think about when using this book:

- Set aside a special place in your home for grammar practice. Keep the area neat, with the book and favorite writing implements close at hand.
- Set up a particular time of day to work on practice pages. This establishes consistency.
- Make sure your child understands the written instructions at the top of each practice page.
- Keep all practice sessions with your child positive. If your child becomes frustrated, set the book aside for a period of time and come back to it later.
- Review the work your child has done.
- Pay attention to those areas in which your child has the most difficulty. Provide extra guidance and further practice in those areas.

Complete Sentences

A complete sentence contains a **subject** and a **predicate**.

☞ The **subject** tells who or what the sentence is about.
   Examples: *My pet rat* likes to eat cheese.
   The tree blew over in the wind.

☞ The **predicate** tells what the subject is or does. The verb is found in the predicate.
   Examples: Jimmy *rode* his bike across California.
   That stray dog *is old and dirty*.

Look at the sentences below. Circle the subject, and underline the predicate.

1. Coyotes and raccoons roam the streets at night.

2. Her mother's car has a dent in it.

3. Tania loves to ice skate.

4. Washington, D.C., has many interesting museums.

5. That family plays board games every Friday night.

6. Mother's Day falls on the second Sunday in May.

7. The students worked on their school yearbook.

8. Oranges are packed with vitamin C.

9. The tree is losing its leaves.

10. Martin lives in England.

11. Apples are good to eat.

12. Italy is a wonderful place to visit.

13. Michael played drums.

14. The fifth-graders studied the environment.

15. He wore a yellow rain jacket and boots.

Complete Sentences *(cont.)*

Now, write 10 complete sentences of your own. Circle each subject and underline each predicate.

1. _____

   _____

2. _____

   _____

3. _____

   _____

4. _____

   _____

5. _____

   _____

6. _____

   _____

7. _____

   _____

8. _____

   _____

9. _____

   _____

10. _____

   _____

Nouns

There are two types of **nouns**:

- **Common nouns** describe a person, place, or thing. They are not capitalized.

    Examples: *The boy* combed his hair. (*person*)

    The city gets cold in the winter. (*place*)

    The cartoon is funny. (*thing*)

- **Proper nouns** describe a specific person, place, or thing and are capitalized.

    Examples: *Johnny Smith* combed his hair. (*person*)

    New York City gets cold in the winter. (*place*)

    The Simpsons is funny. (*thing*)

Change the underlined common nouns below into proper nouns by rewriting each sentence.

1. The movie had me on the edge of my seat. _____

    _____

2. That baseball team lost every game this season. _____

    _____

3. The woman ate a hot fudge sundae. _____

    _____

4. That country is a beautiful place to visit. _____

    _____

5. The song makes me want to dance. _____

    _____

Now, change the underlined proper nouns into common nouns. Rewrite each sentence.

6. Felix likes to play checkers. _____

    _____

7. Broadway Market offers free samples of cheese on Fridays. _____

    _____

8. My brother watches *Sesame Street* in the afternoon. _____

    _____

9. Aunt Sally ran a marathon last summer. _____

    _____

10. Mom and I drank Coca-Cola at the ball game. _____

    _____

Plural Nouns

A **plural noun** indicates more than one person, place, or thing.

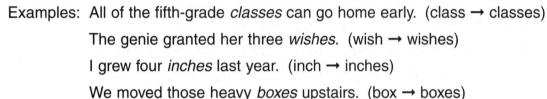

- To form the plural of most nouns, simply add an *s*.

    Examples: The *bears* ate the picnic lunch.

    Those *lawyers* work long hours.

Here are some other rules for forming plural nouns:

- To form the plural of nouns ending in *s*, *sh*, *ch*, or *x*, add *es*.

    Examples: All of the fifth-grade *classes* can go home early. (class → classes)

    The genie granted her three *wishes*. (wish → wishes)

    I grew four *inches* last year. (inch → inches)

    We moved those heavy *boxes* upstairs. (box → boxes)

- To form the plural of nouns ending in the consonant *y*, change the *y* to *i* and add *es*.

    Examples: They visited four *cities* in Europe this summer. (city → cities)

    Those *ladies* collected food for hungry children. (lady → ladies)

- To form the plural of nouns ending with a *vowel + y*, add an *s*.

    Examples: There was a crowd around the *monkeys* at the zoo. (monkey → monkeys)

    In college, you will write many *essays*. (essay → essays)

Write the plural form beside the singular nouns below.

1. cow _____

2. baby _____

3. match _____

4. fox _____

5. turkey _____

6. candle _____

7. party _____

8. dress _____

9. lily _____

10. cry _____

11. wish _____

12. city _____

13. alligator _____

14. crutch _____

15. key _____

16. soda _____

17. hex _____

18. web _____

19. lunch _____

20. dish _____

Plural Nouns *(cont.)*

Here are a few more rules for making singular nouns plural:

- Add an *s* to most nouns ending in *f*.

    Examples: The *chiefs* met for a conference. (chief → chiefs)

    The news *briefs* were short but interesting. (brief → briefs)

- In some cases, change the *f* or *fe* to *v* and add *s*.

    Examples: Many of the *wives* went shopping. (wife → wives)

    Wolves have migrated back to Oregon recently. (wolf → wolves)

- In most compound words, make the main word plural.

    Examples: The *fathers-in-law* sat on the right side of the church.

    Those *passers-by* didn't see the raccoon in the tree.

- Some nouns change their spelling when they become plural.

    Examples: child to *children*, goose to *geese*, man to *men*, tooth to *teeth*, mouse to *mice*

- Some nouns have the same form whether they are singular or plural.

    Examples: *swine, deer, series, sheep, species*

Write the plural form beside the singular nouns below.

1. belief _____

2. goose _____

3. sister-in-law _____

4. wolf _____

5. man_____

6. sheep _____

7. passer-by _____

8. foot_____

9. deer_____

10. chief _____

11. commander-in-chief_____

12. leaf _____

13. dirt _____

14. thief _____

15. father-in-law_____

Pronouns

A **pronoun** is a word used in the place of a noun or another pronoun.

> Examples: I, me, my, we, us, our, ours *(first-person)*
>
> you, your, yours *(second-person)*
>
> he, him, his, she, hers, it, they, them, their, theirs, its *(third-person)*

Use pronouns to avoid repetition in your writing.

◆ *Repetitious sentence:* Mrs. Catchatori gave Mrs. Catchatori's car to Mrs. Catchatori's husband, Mr. Catchatori. Mr. Catchatori loved the car.

◆ *Revised sentence with pronouns:* Mrs. Catchatori gave her car to her husband. He loved it.

Read the story below. Cross out repetitious nouns when needed, and write the appropriate pronoun above it.

The Tamale Party

Juan wanted to teach Juan's friends how to make tamales. He called up Joe, Katie, and Frieda and asked Joe, Katie, and Frieda to come to Juan's house. Joe, Katie, and Frieda arrived at Juan's house on Friday afternoon, and Joe, Katie, and Frieda were so excited! First, Juan showed Juan's friends how to soak cornhusks. Then, Juan smeared masa on one husk while Joe, Katie, and Frieda watched. Finally, Juan placed a spoonful of meat that Juan had cooked in the center of the masa and rolled the cornhusk up into a tamale. Juan's friends were so impressed with Juan. They each took turns making a tamale. At first, Joe's, Katie's, and Frieda's tamales were messy, but with practice, Joe's, Katie's, and Frieda's tamales grew neater. Juan and Juan's friends waited and waited for the tamales to be finished. When the tamales were finished cooking, the tamales smelled so good. Juan, Joe, Katie, and Frieda ate three tamales each.

Pronoun Agreement

Pronouns must agree with their **antecedents**—the words to which they refer.

Example: *Cathy* will borrow a flashlight, which *she* needs to go spelunking.

The **antecedent** is *Cathy*. The **pronoun** is *she*. Therefore, *she* refers to *Cathy*.

Pronouns must match their antecedents in the following ways:

- Number—**My fish and my turtle** both love **their** snack of mealworms.
  (antecedent)   (pronoun)

- Person—If **anyone** wants cake, **he or she** had better come to the cafeteria now.
  (antecedent)   (pronoun)

- Gender—**Martin** gave **his** calculator to his mother.
  (antecedent)   (pronoun)

Look at the sentences below. Fill in the correct pronoun that agrees with the underlined antecedent.

1. <u>Each police officer</u> should wear _____ badge to the dinner.

2. <u>Louise</u> wants to donate _____ old clothes to the homeless.

3. <u>Mom and Dad</u> can't wait to see the photos from _____ vacation.

4. <u>Everybody</u> needs to take out _____ pencil and get to work!

5. <u>The eagle and her babies</u> shared _____ nest with an owl.

6. <u>Jimmy</u> and _____ grandfather love to surf.

7. <u>Maya and Juanita</u> look forward to _____ weekend.

8. <u>Every actor</u> must pay for _____ own makeup and costume.

9. <u>Robert</u> carried _____ baby sister on his back.

10. <u>The ducks</u> swam happily in _____ pond.

Verbs

Verbs are words that name an action or describe a state of being.

There are three basic types of verbs:

◆ **Action verbs** show what someone or something does; they often show some kind of action.

Examples: Molly *laughed* at the comedian.

The truck *rolled* downhill.

◆ **Linking verbs** help the words at the end of a sentence describe the subject.

Examples: Aunt Suzie *is* my mother's cousin.

The clown *was* happy all the time.

◆ **Helping verbs** are added to another verb to make the meaning clearer.

Examples: They *will* run at lunchtime.

She *could* play the piano tonight.

Study the sentences below. In the space beside each sentence, write which type of verb is being used.

1. Jane and Melissa were excited about the party. _____

2. He was studying until midnight. _____

3. The horse galloped around the ring. _____

4. Aunt Joe will write to me from Spain. _____

5. That baby cries all night. _____

6. We are sad that our grandmother broke her hip. _____

Now, write six sentences of your own, using the type of verb listed.

1. **(action verb)** _____

_____

2. **(linking verb)** _____

_____

3. **(helping verb)** _____

_____

4. **(action verb)** _____

_____

5. **(linking verb)** _____

_____

6. **(helping verb)** _____

_____

Past and Present Verb Tenses

Verb tenses are used to show the passing of time. There are several verb tenses, but this lesson will focus on just two—**past** and **present**.

- **Present tense verbs** show that the action is happening to the subject right now.

    Examples: Mr. Jasper *is talking* on the telephone.

    I *am enjoying* pancakes this morning.

    Kathryn and Maxine *are cooking* spaghetti.

- **Past tense verbs** show that the action already happened to the subject.

    Examples: We *climbed* the mountain last Tuesday.

    Dr. Hubert *was disappointed* with the election results.

    My parents *enjoyed* the band's performance.

- Some verbs do not end in *ed* when put into past tense. They are called irregular verbs.

    Examples: present tense—*go*   past tense—*went*

    present tense—*hide*   past tense—*hid*

    present tense—*bring*   past tense—*brought*

Part I: Put the following present tense verbs into past tense. Watch out for irregular verbs!

1. sew _____

2. speak _____

3. watch _____

4. fly _____

5. is _____

6. look _____

7. taste _____

8. call _____

9. cry _____

10. ride _____

Sometimes, other words in the sentence can give clues as to which tense the verb should be in. Words such as *yesterday*, *last month*, and *previously* show that the action occurred in the past. Verbs in the same sentence often share the same tense.

Part II: Study the sentences below. Add a verb on each line provided, making sure that it is in the appropriate tense.

1. Last week, we _____ kickball.

2. Today, I _____ exhausted, and I keep yawning.

3. In 1776, the Declaration of Independence _____ written.

4. Shirley _____ when the performers take a bow.

5. Tonight, Miss Tigard will skate quickly; her cousin _____ very slowly.

Subject and Verb Agreement

Subjects may be singular or plural. The verb form must agree with the subject.

Examples: *Incorrect—Ivan are* going to the store.

Correct—Ivan is going to the store.

Incorrect—We was calling out the cat's name.

Correct—We were calling out the cat's name.

Use the following steps to make sure your verb agrees with your subject:

1. Find the subject of the sentence.
2. Decide whether the subject is singular or plural.
3. Select the appropriate verb form to match the subject.

Study the story below. Cross out inappropriate verb forms and write the correct verb forms above them.

Mr. Fisher and his students is studying ecology. First, they learned that they should never throws our trash into the river. Birds and fish can gets strangled in plastic six-pack rings. They can also chokes on cigarette butts. Each student had a chance to looks into a bird's nest to see the tiny eggs inside. Mr. Fisher explained that bugs eats the poison farmers put on their plants. Then birds gobbles up the bugs and gets poisoned, too. Sometimes, their eggshells is so thin that their babies don't hatch. The students learns a lot that day about how to care for the Earth. When Sara went home, she tells her parents that they need to build a birdhouse. "We already recycles," her father said. "Now, we should plants a garden."

Sentence Fragments

Sentence fragments occur when a sentence is missing either a subject or a verb. This is also called an incomplete sentence.

Examples: *Incorrect*—going to the circus tomorrow.

Problem—Who is going to the circus? The sentence is missing a subject.

Correction—Judy and Flanders are going to the circus tomorrow.

Incorrect—My two cats, Iago and Alger.

Problem—What action is occurring? The sentence is missing a verb.

Correction—My two cats, Iago and Alger, love to sleep in the laundry basket together.

Part I: Study the sentences below. Decide whether each sentence is missing a subject or a verb. Write "subject" or "verb" in the space beside each sentence.

1. camping at the national park _____

2. Reverend Johnson _____

3. is a really good guitar player _____

4. Abraham Lincoln _____

5. can babysit this Friday night _____

6. were hoping to win first prize _____

7. the spotted cow _____

8. Washington, D.C. _____

9. aren't going to be there tonight _____

10. my skateboard _____

Part II: Now, rewrite each fragment, adding either a subject or a verb to make a complete sentence.

1. _____

2. _____

3. _____

4. _____

5. _____

6. _____

7. _____

8. _____

9. _____

10. _____

Adjectives

Adjectives are words that describe either nouns or pronouns. They answer the questions: What kind? How many? Which one? How much?

> Examples: She wore a ring. *(What kind?)*
> She wore a *silver* ring in her nose.
> We served dinner to people. *(How many?)*
> We served dinner to *forty* people.
> Thomas gave a dollar to the man. *(Which one?)*
> Thomas gave a dollar to the *homeless* man.
> I need to buy sugar. *(How much?)*
> I need to buy *three* pounds of sugar.

Part I: Rewrite the following sentences, adding adjectives to answer the questions below.

1. Nathan likes to watch the game on television. *(What kind?)* _____

   _____

2. Fifth-graders crowded the gymnasium. *(How many?)* _____

   _____

3. She rescued the dog. *(Which one?)* _____

   _____

4. Father paid me for sweeping the driveway. *(How much?)* _____

   _____

There are three types of adjectives:

★ **Common adjectives** describe nouns or pronouns.
   Example: He is a *handsome* boy.

★ **Proper adjectives** are formed from proper nouns.
   Example: My uncle loves to eat *Italian* food.

★ **Compound adjectives** are made up of more than one word.
   Examples: My brother is in his *teenage* years.
   The Nor

Part II: Add adjectives to the sentences below according to the type listed after each sentence.

1. My _____ sister loves to dance. *(common adjective)*
2. Tacos and burritos are my favorite _____ food. *(proper adjective)*
3. A submarine is an _____ vehicle. *(compound adjective)*
4. Every Christmas, Uncle Steve brings us _____ oranges. *(proper adjective)*
5. Her _____ roller blades lost a wheel. *(common adjective)*
6. They love to dance to _____ music. *(proper adjective)*
7. The _____ police officer wore a coat and dark glasses. *(compound adjective)*
8. Julie's _____ dog ate her sock. *(common adjective)*
9. I'm going west to soak up the _____ sunshine. *(proper adjective)*
10. Aunt Millie's _____ hair hung to her waist. *(common adjective)*

Adjectives *(cont.)*

Write a one-page story in which you use all of the adjectives in the box below.

beautiful	furry	curly	nearby
striped	twelve	enormous	drenched
silly	Japanese	older	million

_____

_____

_____

_____

_____

_____

_____

_____

_____

_____

_____

_____

_____

_____

_____

_____

_____

_____

_____

Adverbs

Adverbs are words that describe verbs, adjectives, or other adverbs. They answer the questions: When? Where? To what extent? How?

Examples: My best friend moved. *(When?)*
My best friend moved *first*.
The sock fell. *(Where?)*
The sock fell *behind* my dresser.
Maribelle sang. *(How?)*
Maribelle sang *badly*.
The caterpillar ate the leaf. *(To what extent?)*
The caterpillar *partially* ate the leaf.

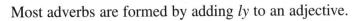

Most adverbs are formed by adding *ly* to an adjective.

Examples: **Adjectives**   **Adverbs**
soft   softly
sad   sadly
beautiful   beautifully

Other adverbs do not end in *ly*.

Examples: already   now   almost
           more   often   yesterday
           far   soon   ahead

Part I: Rewrite the following sentences, adding adverbs to answer the questions below.

1. Susan and Michelle danced. *(When?)* _____

2. The balloon flew. *(Where?)* _____

3. Sparky, Julie's dog, barked. *(How?)*_____

4. I understood the instructions. *(To what extent?)* _____

Part II: Add adverbs to the sentences below to correspond with the question after each sentence.

1. Matthew studied _____ for the test. *(How?)*

2. Mrs. Sawyer left _____ for Europe. *(When?)*

3. The houseplants grew _____ in that dark room. *(How?)*

4. Move _____ to the front of the line. *(Where?)*

5. We woke up _____ and walked the dog. *(When?)*

6. She ran _____ down the hill. *(How?)*

7. We are _____ finished with our homework. *(To what extent?)*

8. Go _____ to the basement and find the flashlight. *(How?)*

9. I like to read my library books _____. *(When?)*

10. They played football _____. *(To what extent?)*

Adverbs *(cont.)*

Write a one-page story in which you use all of the adverbs in the box below.

unbelievably	afterward	eagerly	gracefully
clearly	slowly	loudly	sadly
carefully	tomorrow	more	happily

_____

_____

_____

_____

_____

_____

_____

_____

_____

_____

_____

_____

_____

_____

_____

_____

_____

_____

_____

_____

Prepositions

Prepositions are words that link a noun or pronoun following it to another word in the sentence. Here is a list of some of the most common prepositions:

above	at	from	out	under
across	behind	in	over	until
after	beneath	inside	outside	up
along	between	of	through	with
around	during	on	toward	

Part I: Circle the prepositions in the following sentences.

1. Great-horned owls live in abandoned nests.

2. Sometimes they live inside dead trees.

3. Other times, they nest on cliffs.

4. You can find owl pellets beneath their nests.

5. There are bones and feathers inside the pellets.

6. During the time that the owls are babies, their parents bring them food.

7. After several months, the baby owls are ready to fly.

8. They venture out of the nest cautiously.

9. You can observe Great-horned owls at night.

10. Watch out if one flies toward you!

Part II: Now, add prepositions to complete the following sentences.

1. To get to the fort, you must crawl _____ a fence.

2. Then you have to climb _____ a hill.

3. _____ the cow pasture, you'll see a yellow mailbox.

4. Walk _____ you spot a tree marked with an X.

5. _____ the tree, you'll find a wooden crate.

6. Climb _____ top of the crate and grab the lowest tree branch.

7. Once you're _____ the tree, you're almost there.

8. Look up, and you'll see the fort _____ you.

9. Pull yourself _____ to the front door.

10. Prepare to walk _____ the fort!

Prepositions *(cont.)*

In a creative and interesting paragraph, describe how to get from your house to your school. Use as many prepositions as you can in your 10- to 12-sentence description.

After you are finished with your paragraph, circle the prepositions. How many did you use?

Putting It All Together I

Use the following parts of speech to create 10 new sentences. You can change the forms of the words (tense, singular to plural), as needed. Try not to use any word twice.

Nouns	Verbs	Adjectives	Adverbs	Prepositions
Dr. Hansen	kick	lavender	neatly	above
soccer ball	slide	salty	tiredly	into
alligator	is	terrifying	excitedly	before
New York City	feel	cold	regretfully	until
apple	munch	painful	tomorrow	over
spider	cry	blue	badly	under
car	spill	angry	merrily	in
anteater	jump	ugly	quietly	on
Mom	scream	silly	happily	beneath
diamond ring	paint	broken	slowly	through

1. _____

_____

2. _____

_____

3. _____

_____

4. _____

_____

5. _____

_____

6. _____

_____

7. _____

_____

8. _____

_____

9. _____

_____

10. _____

_____

Coordinating Conjunctions

A **coordinating conjunction** links two sentences together. When joining two sentences, put a comma before the coordinating conjunction.

> Examples: I like coffee, *but* my mother doesn't allow me to drink it.
> Jarvis is sick, *so* he can't go to the football game.
> She's excited, *for* tomorrow is her birthday.

Here are the seven coordinating conjunctions:

> **f**or   **a**nd   **n**or   **b**ut   **o**r   **y**et   **s**o

When grouped like this, they form a **mnemonic device** (a teaching tool used to remember them) called *fanboys*. A mnemonic often uses the first letter of each word in a list to form a new word that is easy to remember.

Part I: Study the following sentences. Circle the subject, underline the predicate, and draw a box around the coordinating conjunction.

1. The weather is sunny, but soon it will rain.

2. We are going shopping, and we will eat dinner out.

3. Theresa rode her bicycle, so she is breathing hard.

4. Dean planted peas last month, for he loves to garden.

5. My cousin likes chocolate, or maybe she likes caramel.

6. I don't understand geometry, nor do I understand science.

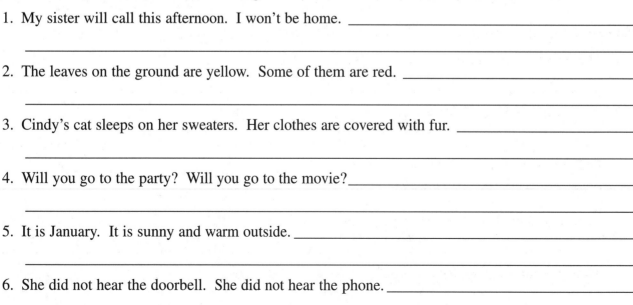

Part II: Now, study the groups of sentences below. Using one of the "fanboys," rewrite each pair of sentences to make one sentence. Don't forget the comma.

1. My sister will call this afternoon. I won't be home. _____

   _____

2. The leaves on the ground are yellow. Some of them are red. _____

   _____

3. Cindy's cat sleeps on her sweaters. Her clothes are covered with fur. _____

   _____

4. Will you go to the party? Will you go to the movie? _____

   _____

5. It is January. It is sunny and warm outside. _____

   _____

6. She did not hear the doorbell. She did not hear the phone. _____

   _____

Run-on Sentences

Run-on sentences occur in one of two ways.

In the first type, the sentence is missing punctuation and/or a coordinating conjunction. Add a period or a comma and a coordinating conjunction to fix it.

> Examples: I went to the dentist I had five cavities. (*run-on*)
>
> I went to the dentist, and I had five cavities. (*correct*)
>
> I went to the dentist. I had five cavities. (*correct*)

Part I: Study the run-on sentences. Rewrite them correctly on the line below.

1. Lydia bought a new dress it is blue _____

   _____

2. Jackie runs three days a week twice a week she lifts weights. _____

   _____

3. The peregrine falcon dove down from the sky it caught a sparrow. _____

   _____

4. The cars raced down the street my dog started barking. _____

   _____

5. Seymour is my uncle he has a long mustache. _____

   _____

In the second type of run-on sentence, the sentence is missing a word or words. Add a word or words to fix it.

> Examples: Harry loves to go snowboarding, he goes every Saturday. (*run-on*)
>
> Harry loves to go snowboarding, so he goes every Saturday. (*correct*)
>
> Harry loves to go snowboarding, and he goes every Saturday. (*correct*)

Part II: Study the run-on sentences. Rewrite them on the line below.

1. The ocean is cold, I swim anyway. _____

   _____

2. It is six o' clock, it is time for dinner. _____

   _____

3. I forgot my umbrella, I'm going to get soaked. _____

   _____

4. Thursday is my birthday, I'm going to Disneyland. _____

   _____

5. Mother is afraid of spiders, she took the black widow outside. _____

   _____

Double Negatives

A **double negative** is a statement that contains two negative descriptive words.

Examples: The girls did *not* have *no* money to buy ice cream. (*double negative*)

The girls did *not* have *any* money to buy ice cream. (*correct*)

He *didn't* say *nothing*. (*double negative*)

He *didn't* say *anything*. (*correct*)

Here are the most frequently used negative descriptive words.

- **no**   - **never**   - **not**   - **none**   - **nothing**

To avoid a double negative, use only one negative word to express a negative idea in a sentence.

Study the sentences below. Underline the negative words in each sentence. Then rewrite the sentences on the lines below to eliminate the double negative.

1. Mrs. O'Connor never got no newspaper today. _____

   _____

2. Nothing in the way of chores never gets done in this house. _____

   _____

3. He is not no good role model for children. _____

   _____

4. None of those muffins is no good. _____

   _____

5. I never got nothing at all for my birthday. _____

   _____

6. No bears better not eat my picnic basket. _____

   _____

7. She's not going to earn no points in the basketball game. _____

   _____

8. I never read no book to teach me how to embroider. _____

   _____

9. Mrs. Jenkins is not no expert at horseback riding. _____

   _____

10. I do not have no talent in singing. _____

   _____

Exclamatory Sentences

Exclamatory sentences show strong emotions. They end with an exclamation point.

Examples: A snake bit me!

Your room is a mess!

There's a horse in the classroom!

Study the following situations. Write exclamatory sentences to describe each one on the lines below. Don't forget the exclamation point!

1. The doorbell rings. You open the door, and there on the doorstep stands your long-lost sister. What do you say? _____

_____

2. You're making cookies. You forget to use a hot-pad, and you reach into the oven and grab the cookie sheet with your bare hand. What do you say? _____

_____

3. You've just purchased a lottery ticket. You scratch off the numbers, look on the television, and find out you're a winner. What do you say?_____

_____

4. You've got five minutes to get to school. Suddenly, you run over glass, and your bike gets a flat tire. What do you say? _____

_____

5. Your mother takes you out shopping for your birthday. You get home to a dark house. Suddenly, the lights go on, and all your friends shout, "Happy Birthday!" What do you say?_____

_____

6. You're running down the sidewalk barefooted. You don't see the uneven cement, and you trip, stubbing your toe and skinning your knees. What do you say?_____

_____

7. You walk into your classroom. Instead of your teacher, you come face to face with a gorilla. What do you say? _____

_____

8. You're walking in the park. Suddenly, you smell something horrible and realize you've stepped in something unpleasant. What do you say? _____

_____

9. You've just cleaned your room and taken out the trash. You're ready to go outside and play when your mom asks you to clean out the refrigerator. What do you say?_____

_____

10. You're eating a triple-dip ice cream cone. Suddenly, one scoop falls in your lap, and the other falls on your dog's head. What do you say?_____

_____

Interrogative Sentences

Interrogative sentences ask a question. They end with a question mark.

Examples: How many ounces are in a quart?

Who was the first president of the United States?

Where is the city of Springfield?

Journalists often use the following question-words when conducting interviews:

• **Who?**   • **What?**   • **Where?**   • **When?**   • **Why?**   • **How?**

Pretend you are interviewing a parent, brother, or sister for a newspaper article about him or her. Write 10 questions you would like to ask this person.

1. _____
2. _____
3. _____
4. _____
5. _____
6. _____
7. _____
8. _____
9. _____
10. _____

Now, ask this person your questions. Write a descriptive paragraph about him or her, incorporating the answers to your questions. Read your paragraph aloud to your family.

_____
_____
_____
_____
_____
_____
_____

Imperative Sentences

Imperative sentences give orders or directions. They end with a period or an exclamation point, depending on the tone of the command.

> Examples: Be quiet and listen!
>
> First, write your name on your paper.

Pretend you are the teacher for a day. Study the following situations below, and write imperative sentences to correspond with each situation.

1. The children are standing on their desks and throwing paper airplanes.

   _____

2. Janey is blowing bubbles with her gum.

   _____

3. You want the class to take a spelling test.

   _____

4. Jeremy keeps getting up to sharpen his pencil.

   _____

5. Michael has brought a cat into the classroom.

   _____

6. It's time for silent reading.

   _____

7. Casey and Tara are talking while you're trying to speak to the class.

   _____

8. Kathy can't stop sneezing.

   _____

9. The bell rings to go home.

   _____

10. Johnny stays after school to give you a bunch of flowers.

    _____

Capitalization

Capital letters are used in all sorts of ways.

In general, capitalize the following:

- Titles of people

    Examples: *Mr.* Jackson wrote a novel.

    I brought *Mom* breakfast in bed.

- Names of towns, counties, countries, and states

    Examples: Yumiko, who lives in *Japan*, is visiting *Washington, D.C.*

    They live in *Eugene*, which is part of *Lane County* in *Oregon*.

- Days of the week and months of the year

    Examples: On *March 5th*, we'll go to the ballet.

    Last *January*, it rained for three weeks straight!

    My birthday is *November 10*, and this year it's on *Tuesday*.

- Street names

    Examples: Joseph lives on *Verde Oak Road*.

    Her house, at 225 *Spring Street*, is difficult to find.

- Names of holidays

    Examples: *Hanukkah* and *Christmas* are celebrated in *December*.

    Will you celebrate *Chinese New Year*?

- The first word of direct quotations, as well as the first word in a sentence

    Examples: *Marvin* touched the hot stove and then he yelled, "*Ouch*!"

    "*Until* you clean your room, you cannot play outside," said Dad.

- The salutation and closing of a letter

    Examples: *Dear* Jorge,

    Sincerely, Margaret

Study the sentences below. Cross out lowercase letters and replace them with capital letters, as needed.

1. aunt carrie lives in bethany, missouri.
2. my dog, marley, loves the snow in alaska.
3. Ms. nadir hopes to travel to europe in july.
4. grandpa lives on friendly street in boston, massachusetts.
5. dear jonathan, Thank you for the flowers you sent last sunday.
6. dr. rozic isn't accepting new patients until december.
7. the girl stared at the spider, and then yelled, "a tarantula!"
8. i hope to see you soon. sincerely, annie
9. we usually celebrate easter in march or april.
10. dad lives in the town of oak view in California.

Capitalization *(cont.)*

Study the words in the box below. Decide which should be capitalized. Cross out incorrect lowercase letters and replace them with capitals. Then write a story in the space below, using all of the words given.

senator jones	ostrich	new mexico
monday	august	trumpet
enchilada	birthday party	birch street
los angeles	halloween	germany
america	uncle rudy	parade

Periods

Use a **period** at the end of a sentence to show where the sentence stops.

Periods are also used in the following ways:

- Initials (She had *J.R.* engraved on her luggage; it stood for Jenny Randall.)
- Titles before names (*Dr.* Josephine loves to ride horses.)
- Abbreviations (You should bring a tent, a sleeping bag, *etc.*, on the trip.)

Part I: Study the sentences below. Add periods where needed.

1. Last Wednesday, Mrs Stevens found a stray cat

2. She examined it for an id tag. It read MB

3. "Mr Stevens, what should we do?" she asked her husband.

4. "Take it to Dr Barnes at the animal hospital," he suggested.

5. Mrs Stevens found the vet on River St and drove over.

6. "Dr Barnes is out today," said the receptionist. "You'll have to see Dr McConnell."

7. Dr. McConnell examined the cat

8. "It looks healthy, Mrs Stevens," he said.

9. Mrs. Stevens put up fliers that said, "Cat found on West 5th Ave"

10. Mr Bates called the next day to claim his beloved cat named "Mrs Boots"

Part II: Abbreviate the following words, making sure to add periods where needed.

1. Avenue _____

2. Street _____

3. Road _____

4. Place _____

5. Mister _____

6. Missus _____

7. Doctor _____

8. etcetera _____

9. identification _____

10. Post Office _____

Commas

You've studied how to use commas with coordinating conjunctions to create a long sentence. Commas are also used in the following ways:

◆ Use a comma when writing out a date.

    Examples: We celebrated the millennium on December 31, 2000.

                 The Declaration of Independence was signed on July 4, 1776.

◆ Use commas to separate the names of geographical locations.

    Examples: My family lives in Taos, New Mexico.

                 Jamie's pen pal is from Tokyo, Japan.

◆ Use a comma after greetings and closings in a letter.

    Examples: Dear Santa Claus, I'd like a pony for Christmas.

                 Affectionately yours, Suzie.

Study the sentences below. Add commas where needed.

1. I've always wanted to see Tucson Arizona.
2. Finally, I left my house in Sheridan Wyoming.
3. I started driving on June 14 2003.
4. I ended up in Tucson on June 19 2003.
5. "Dear Mom" I wrote. "I love the desert."
6. I'm driving up to Phoenix Arizona tomorrow.
7. Wish you were here. Love Sally"
8. I met a woman from Ventura California.
9. We have the same birthday: October 24 1980.

Think of a trip you've been on. In the space below, write a letter to a friend describing your trip. Use at least eight commas. Don't forget to add a greeting and closing.

Putting It All Together II

Study the following sentences and correct the punctuation, as needed.

1. my aunt michele runs a deli in juno alaska.

   _____

2. The deli is located at 21 lincoln st

   _____

3. uncle scott helps aunt michele run the deli

   _____

4. they had a grand opening on july 19 2003.

   _____

5. dr robinson baked a beautiful cake for the occasion

   _____

6. Aunt michele wrote him a letter later, addressed to 41 12th ave

   _____

7. "Dear Dr robinson" she wrote. "thank you for the lovely cake. my husband would like the recipe. sincerely michele"

   _____

8. Now the deli serves chili, sandwiches, cake, etc to hungry customers.

   _____

9. People come from as far away as rome italy to eat at aunt Michele's deli

   _____

10. have you ever been to new york city new york?

    _____

11. I went to a deli there on December 31 2000

    _____

12. Mr soprano owns that deli, so I wrote to him.

    _____

13. "Dear mr Soprano" I wrote. "Thank you for the free bagels They are almost as good as my aunt's. Sincerely Johnny"

    _____

14. one day mr soprano who was on vacation came to aunt michele's deli

    _____

15. we all had a great time visiting sharing recipes and showing him around town.

    _____

Apostrophes in Contractions

Contractions refer to two words that have been combined.

Add an **apostrophe** in the space where a letter or letters have been omitted.

Examples: can + not = can't
you + are = you're
I + am = I'm
were + not = weren't

Part I: Study the words below. Write the contraction beside them, making sure to add an apostrophe. Finally, write the letters that were omitted during the contraction. The first one has been done for you.

1. I + will =   I'll   wi
2. should + not = _____ _____
3. we + are = _____ _____
4. she + is = _____ _____
5. they + are = _____ _____
6. I + am = _____ _____
7. could + not = _____ _____
8. can + not = _____ _____
9. you + will = _____ _____
10. he + will = _____ _____
11. I + would = _____ _____
12. he + is = _____ _____
13. you + are = _____ _____
14. she + had = _____ _____

Part II: Change the underlined words in the sentences below into contractions. Don't forget to add apostrophes.

1. <u>They will</u> be here at eight P.M. _____
2. My sister <u>should not</u> be late. _____
3. We <u>can not</u> wait for her. _____
4. <u>She is</u> often late for dinner. _____
5. <u>I am</u> tired of waiting for her. _____
6. Tonight, <u>she will</u> be on time, I am sure of it. _____
7. <u>They are</u> right on time. _____
8. <u>We will</u> wait in the living room. _____
9. <u>There is</u> a knock on the door. _____
10. <u>It is</u> my sister, five minutes late. _____
11. "<u>We are</u> ready to go!" I told her. _____
12. "<u>I will</u> just grab a snack," she said. _____
13. "<u>You will</u> make us even later!" I replied. _____
14. <u>We would</u> have seen the play if it hadn't been for her. _____
15. "You <u>must not</u> be late ever again," I said.

Apostrophes in Possessives

Possessives are words that show ownership. The apostrophe is placed before adding *s*.

Examples: Mary's dog (*the dog belonging to Mary*)
Uncle Junior's son (*the son belonging to Uncle Junior*)
JoJo's house (*the house belonging to JoJo*)

Part I: Rewrite the following phrases to make possessives. Don't forget the apostrophe. The first one has been done for you.

1. a drum set belonging to Jill _____Jill's drum set_____
2. the photos belonging to John _____
3. the canary belonging to Aunt Lisa _____
4. a car belonging to Mom _____
5. the gift belonging to my friend _____
6. a desk belonging to that teacher _____
7. the dictionary belonging to Cathy _____
8. the foot belonging to Mike _____
9. the dishes belonging to Grandma _____
10. the film projector belonging to that classroom _____
11. the mug belonging to Father _____
12. the cat belonging to Grandpa _____
13. the money belonging to the state _____
14. the yard belonging to the house _____
15. the passengers belonging to the airplane _____

Part II: Study the sentences below. Add apostrophes to the possessives, as needed.

1. I borrowed Uncle Tonys shovel.
2. I needed it to work in Mothers garden.
3. The dirts consistency was rocky.
4. I put on my aunts gloves.
5. I wore my mothers floppy hat.
6. The suns heat beat down on me.
7. I planted my sisters tomato seedlings.
8. Californias weather is good for growing tomatoes.
9. My mothers tomatoes looked healthy.
10. Suddenly, the shovel was in my dogs mouth.
11. The scarecrows face looked amused.
12. My uncles face looked angry.
13. I bought him a new shovel from our towns hardware store.
14. I also bought the stores best dog leash.
15. My dogs howls woke the earthworms when I put him on his new leash.

34

Apostrophes in Contractions and Possessives

Study the pairs of words below. Label one a contraction, and the other a possessive. Then use both words in a sentence. The first one has been done for you.

1. can't _____ contraction _____

   grandmother's _____ possessive _____

   I can't find my grandmother's watch.

2. Jennifer's _____

   she'll _____

   _____

3. we'll _____

   sister's _____

   _____

4. elephant's _____

   should've _____

   _____

5. restaurant's _____

   won't _____

   _____

6. I'm _____

   president's _____

   _____

7. you'll _____

   Washington's _____

   _____

8. horse's _____

   they'll _____

   _____

9. haven't _____

   Freddie's _____

   _____

10. yesterday's _____

    didn't _____

    _____

Quotation Marks

Quotation marks should be used any time someone speaks. One set of quotation marks should be placed at the beginning of the quote and one set at the end.

> Examples: "Hark, who goes there?" he asked in the darkened room.
>
> Cindy ran into the classroom and yelled, "It's snowing!"
>
> "I like you," he said, "and I hope you like me."

Study the sentences below. Add quotation marks where needed.

1. When will you be home? Louise asked her mother.

2. Mom thought a moment, then replied, Very soon.

3. Can you pick up some milk, Louise said, if you're stopping at the store?

4. Sure, Mom said. I'll buy eggs, too.

5. Thank you, replied Louise.

6. Mom hung up, then called back. I love you, she said.

7. I love you, too, Louise answered.

8. Drive safely, she added.

9. Mom laughed. Of course, she said.

10. Louise ended the call by saying, Goodbye.

Now, write a conversation between two kids who are talking about a friend's birthday party. Write at least 10 sentences. Make sure to use quotation marks, as needed.

_____

_____

_____

_____

_____

_____

_____

_____

_____

Colons

The **colon** is used between hours and minutes when you are writing out the time.

Examples: At *2:30* A.M., you'll be able to see the meteor shower.

They were married at exactly *1:30* P.M.

He woke up and looked at the clock; it said *3:30*.

Study the sentences below. Rewrite each sentence on the lines below, adding colons where needed.

1. Bill woke up at 630 this morning. _____

    _____

2. He hoped to make the 710 bus _____

    _____

3. At 700, he spilled coffee on his white shirt. _____

    _____

4. At 710, his dog brought a muddy bone into the house. _____

    _____

5. Bill put the dog in the bathtub at 720._____

    _____

6. He missed the bus at 810. _____

    _____

7. Bill didn't get to work until 914._____

    _____

8. "Work starts at 830!" his boss yelled. _____

    _____

9. "I woke up at 630," Bill stammered. _____

    _____

10. His boss cried, "Next time, wake up at 530!" _____

    _____

Putting It All Together III
Writing a Letter

Choose a partner. Using what you have learned about punctuation, write your partner a letter about your life. When you are finished with your letter, give it to your partner to check for correct spelling, grammar, and punctuation. Have your partner circle any errors he/she finds.

_____
(date)

_____
(greeting)

_____

_____

_____

_____

_____

_____

_____

_____

_____

_____

_____

_____

(closing) _____

(signature) _____

Putting It All Together III
Writing a Letter *(cont.)*

Now, write the final draft of your letter, correcting any spelling, punctuation, and grammatical errors. When you are finished, read it to the class!

Assessment

Fill in the bubble in front of the correct answer for each group of possible answers.

1. Those gooses have white bodies and black heads.
   - (A) Those geeses have white bodies and black heads.
   - (B) Those geese have white bodies and black heads.
   - (C) Those goose have white bodies and black heads.
   - (D) Correct as is

2. We took the bus to the museum.
   - (A) We takes the bus to the museum.
   - (B) We tooked the bus to the museum.
   - (C) We taken the bus to the museum.
   - (D) Correct as is

3. Until you finish your homework.
   - (A) Until you finish your homework, you must stay in.
   - (B) Until you finish your homework and the dishes.
   - (C) Until you finish your homework,
   - (D) Correct as is

4. She sang so beautiful.
   - (A) She sang so beautifulness.
   - (B) She sang so beautifuling.
   - (C) She sang so beautifully.
   - (D) Correct as is

5. We walked to the store, and we bought snacks.
   - (A) We walked to the store and we bought snacks.
   - (B) We walked, to the store and we bought snacks.
   - (C) We walked to the store and we, bought snacks.
   - (D) Correct as is

6. Trina is a smart girl she likes to read the dictionary.
   - (A) Trina is a smart girl, and she likes to read the dictionary.
   - (B) Trina is a smart girl and she likes to read the dictionary.
   - (C) Trina is a smart girl. she likes to read the dictionary.
   - (D) Correct as is

7. The truck rumbled over the road, it bounced over rocks.
   - (A) The truck rumbled over the road. it bounced over rocks.
   - (B) The truck rumbled over the road, yet it bounced over rocks.
   - (C) The truck rumbled over the road, and it bounced over rocks.
   - (D) Correct as is

Assessment *(cont.)*

8. He doesn't have any money for the movie.
   (A) He doesn't have no money for the movie.
   (B) He doesn't have none money for the movie.
   (C) He doesn't have nothing money for the movie.
   (D) Correct as is

9. Look out for that falling tree?
   (A) Look out for that falling tree.
   (B) Look out for that falling tree!
   (C) Look out for that falling tree,
   (D) Correct as is

10. Where were you last Sunday night.
    (A) Where were you last Sunday night?
    (B) Where were you last Sunday night!
    (C) Where were you last Sunday night,
    (D) Correct as is

11. Mrs. norton loves palm beach.
    (A) Mrs. Norton loves palm Beach.
    (B) Mrs. Norton loves Palm beach.
    (C) Mrs. Norton loves Palm Beach.
    (D) Correct as is

12. Dr Samuel works on Fifth Ave above a market.
    (A) Dr. Samuel works on Fifth Ave above a market.
    (B) Dr. Samuel works on Fifth. Ave above a market.
    (C) Dr. Samuel works on Fifth Ave. above a market.
    (D) Correct as is

13. My best friend lives in Redondo Beach, California.
    (A) My best friend lives in Redondo Beach California.
    (B) My best friend lives in Redondo Beach. California.
    (C) My best friend lives in, Redondo Beach California.
    (D) Correct as is

14. Dear Johnny. Where is the car?
    (A) Dear Johnny, Where is the car?
    (B) Dear Johnny Where is the car?
    (C) Dear Johnny? Where is the car?
    (D) Correct as is

Assessment *(cont.)*

15. Children shouldnt play with matches.
    - (A) Children should'nt play with matches.
    - (B) Children shouldnt' play with matches.
    - (C) Children shouldn't play with matches.
    - (D) Correct as is

16. That is my grandmothers surfboard.
    - (A) That is my grandmothers' surfboard.
    - (B) That is my grandmother's surfboard.
    - (C) That is my grandmothers's surfboard.
    - (D) Correct as is

17. Stop, thief! cried the banker.
    - (A) "Stop, thief! cried the banker.
    - (B) "Stop," thief! cried the banker.
    - (C) "Stop, thief!" cried the banker.
    - (D) Correct as is

18. Each student should wear his or her nametag.
    - (A) Each student should wear their nametag.
    - (B) Each student should wear its nametag.
    - (C) Each student should wear thems nametag.
    - (D) Correct as is

19. Yesterday, Jackie and Mike walk a mile.
    - (A) Yesterday, Jackie and Mike walks a mile.
    - (B) Yesterday, Jackie and Mike walking a mile.
    - (C) Yesterday, Jackie and Mike walked a mile.
    - (D) Correct as is

20. The cat with the dirty face
    - (A) The cat with the dirty face ate chicken.
    - (B) The cat with the dirty face!
    - (C) The cat with the dirty face and paws
    - (D) Correct as is

21. Run quickly away from that monster!
    - (A) Run quick away from that monster!
    - (B) Run quickedly away from that monster!
    - (C) Run quicking away from that monster!
    - (D) Correct as is

Assessment *(cont.)*

22. Put your pencil in the table.
    - (A) Put your pencil on the table.
    - (B) Put your pencil into the table.
    - (C) Put your pencil before the table.
    - (D) Correct as is

23. She likes to draw. and she likes to paint.
    - (A) She likes to draw, and she likes to paint.
    - (B) She likes to draw and, she likes to paint.
    - (C) She likes to, draw and she likes to paint.
    - (D) Correct as is

24. Marty played guitar, Adam played drums.
    - (A) Marty played guitar. But Adam, played drums.
    - (B) Marty played guitar Adam played drums.
    - (C) Marty played guitar, and Adam played drums.
    - (D) Correct as is

25. Mrs. Holman doesn't have nothing to eat.
    - (A) Mrs. Holman don't have nothing to eat.
    - (B) Mrs. Holman has nothing to eat.
    - (C) Mrs. Holman didn't have nothing to eat.
    - (D) Correct as is

26. Look out for the shark?
    - (A) Look out for the shark!
    - (B) Look out for the shark.
    - (C) Look out! for the shark.
    - (D) Correct as is

27. Who is bringing cookies to the sale?
    - (A) Who is bringing cookies to the sale!
    - (B) Who is bringing cookies to the sale.
    - (C) Who is bringing cookies to the sale
    - (D) Correct as is

28. seattle is located in washington.
    - (A) Seattle is located in washington.
    - (B) Seattle is located in Washington.
    - (C) seattle is located in Washington.
    - (D) Correct as is

29. Thank you for the lovely dinner. Sincerely, Nell

    Ⓐ Thank you for the lovely dinner, Sincerely, Nell

    Ⓑ Thank you for the lovely dinner. Sincerely. Nell.

    Ⓒ Thank you for the lovely dinner, Sincerely. Nell

    Ⓓ Correct as is

30. That's Susans bicycle.

    Ⓐ Thats Susans bicycle.

    Ⓑ That's Susans bicycle.

    Ⓒ That's Susan's bicycle.

    Ⓓ Correct as is

31. I can't get no answer to my question.

    Ⓐ I cannot get no answer to my question.

    Ⓑ I can't get an answer to my question.

    Ⓒ I can't get nothing answer to my question.

    Ⓓ Correct as is

32. She walked slowly to the baseball field.

    Ⓐ She walked slow to the baseball field.

    Ⓑ She walked slower to the baseball field.

    Ⓒ She walked slowlying to the baseball field.

    Ⓓ Correct as is

33. We love the theater in Chicago, illinois.

    Ⓐ We love the theater in Chicago Illinois.

    Ⓑ We love the theater in chicago, illinois.

    Ⓒ We love the theater in Chicago, Illinois.

    Ⓓ correct as is

34. Take your hand off that knife immediately?

    Ⓐ Take your hand off that knife immediately!

    Ⓑ Take your hand off that knife immediately,

    Ⓒ Take your hand off that knife "immediately."

    Ⓓ Correct as is

35. We go to the store yesterday.

    Ⓐ We going to the store yesterday.

    Ⓑ We went to the store yesterday.

    Ⓒ We goes to the store yesterday.

    Ⓓ Correct as is

Assessment *(cont.)*

36. Jane is a prettiest girl.
    A. Jane is a prettying girl.
    B. Jane is a more pretty girl.
    C. Jane is a pretty girl.
    D. Correct as is

37. "Come over here!" I shouted.
    A. "Come over here! I shouted.
    B. Come over here! I shouted.
    C. "Come over here" I shouted.
    D. Correct as is

38. Aunt Nancy was born on March 2 1956.
    A. Aunt Nancy was born on March 2, 1956.
    B. Aunt Nancy was born on March 2. 1956.
    C. Aunt Nancy was born on: March 2 1956.
    D. Correct as is

39. The time is 405 P.M.
    A. The time is 40:5 P.M.
    B. The time is 4:05 P.M.
    C. The time is :405 P.M.
    D. Correct as is

40. Those mousses got out of their cage.
    A. Those mices got out of their cage.
    B. Those mouse got out of their cage.
    C. Those mice got out of their cage.
    D. Correct as is

41. We would'nt be ready on time.
    A. We wouldnt' be ready on time.
    B. We would n't be ready on time.
    C. We wouldn't be ready on time.
    D. Correct as is

42. Thank you for the award. Sincerely, Laura
    A. Thank you for the award, sincerely, Laura
    B. Thank you for the award, Sincerely. Laura
    C. Thank you for the award. Sincerely. Laura.
    D. Correct as is

Answer Key

Page 4
1. (Coyotes and raccoons) roam the streets at night.
2. (Her mother's car) has a dent in it.
3. (Tania) loves to ice skate
4. (Washington, D.C.) has many interesting museums.
5. (That family) plays board games every Friday night.
6. (Mother's Day) falls on the second Sunday in May.
7. (The students) worked on their school yearbook.
8. (Oranges) are packed with Vitamin C.
9. (The tree) is losing its leaves.
10. (Martin) lives in England.
11. (Apples) are good to eat
12. (Italy) is a wonderful place to visit.
13. (Michael) played drums.
14. (The fifth-graders) studied the environment.
15. (He) wore a yellow rain jacket and boots.

Page 5
Answers will vary.

Page 6
1.–5. Answers will vary.
6. That boy
7. The market
8. the show
9. The girl
10. soda

Page 7
1. cows
2. babies
3. matches
4. foxes
5. turkeys
6. candles
7. parties
8. dresses
9. lilies
10. cries
11. wishes
12. cities
13. alligators
14. crutches
15. keys
16. sodas
17. hexes
18. webs
19. lunches
20. dishes

Page 8
1. beliefs
2. geese
3. sisters-in-law
4. wolves
5. men
6. sheep
7. passersby
8. feet
9. deer
10. chiefs
11. commanders-in-chief
12. leaves
13. dirt
14. thieves
15. fathers-in-law

Page 9
Juan wanted to teach <u>his</u> friends how to make tamales. He called up Joe, Katie, and Frieda and asked <u>them</u> to come to <u>his</u> house. Joe, Katie, and Frieda arrived at his house on Friday afternoon, and <u>they</u> were so excited! First, Juan showed <u>his</u> friends how to soak cornhusks. Then, <u>he</u> smeared masa on one husk while Joe, Katie, and Frieda watched. Finally, Juan placed a spoonful of meat that <u>he</u> had cooked in the center of the masa and rolled the cornhusk up into a tamale. Juan's friends were so impressed with <u>him</u>. They each took turns making a tamale. At first, <u>their</u> tamales were messy, but with practice, <u>their</u> tamales grew neater. Juan and <u>his</u> friends waited and waited for the tamales to be finished. When the tamales were finished cooking, <u>they</u> smelled so good. Juan, Joe, Katie, and Frieda ate three tamales each.

Page 10
1. his or her
2. her
3. their
4. his or her
5. their
6. his
7. their
8. his or her
9. his
10. their

Page 11
1. linking
2. helping
3. action
4. helping
5. action
6. linking

Page 12
Part I
1. sewed
2. spoke
3. watched
4. flew
5. was
6. looked
7. tasted
8. called
9. cried
10. rode

Part II
1. played
2. am
3. was
4. claps
5. will skate

Page 13
Mr. Fisher and his students <u>are</u> studying ecology. First, they learned that they should never <u>throw</u> our trash into the river. Birds and fish can <u>get</u> strangled in plastic six-pack rings. They can also <u>choke</u> on cigarette butts. Each student had a chance to look into a bird's nest to see the tiny eggs inside. Mr. Fisher explained that bugs <u>eat</u> the poison farmers put on their plants. Then birds <u>gobble</u> up the bugs and get poisoned, too. Sometimes, their eggshells are so thin that their babies don't hatch. The students <u>learned</u> a lot that day about how to care for the Earth. When Sara went home, she <u>told</u> her parents that they need to build a birdhouse. "We already recycle," her father said. "Now, we should <u>plant</u> a garden."

Answer Key (cont.)

Page 14

Part I
1. subject
2. verb
3. subject
4. verb
5. subject
6. subject
7. verb
8. verb
9. subject
10. verb

Pages 15–16
Answers will vary.

Pages 17–18
Answers will vary.

Page 19

Part I
1. in
2. inside
3. on
4. beneath
5. inside
6. During
7. After
8. out
9. at
10. toward

Part II
Answers will vary.

Page 21
Answers will vary.

Page 22
1. (The weather) is sunny, [but] soon it will rain.
2. (We) are going shopping, [and] (we) will eat dinner out.
3. (Theresa) rode her bicycle, [so] (she) is breathing hard.
4. (Dean) planted peas last month, [for] (he) loves to garden.
5. (My cousin) likes chocolate, [or] maybe (she) likes caramel.
6. (I) don't understand geometry, [nor] do (I) understand science.

Page 23
Answers will vary.

Page 24
1. never, no; Mrs. O'Connor never got a newspaper today.
2. nothing, never; Nothing in the way of chores ever gets done in this house.
3. not, no; He is not a good role model for children.
4. none, no; None of those muffins is good.
5. never, nothing; I never got anything for my birthday.
6. no, not; Bears better not eat my picnic basket.
7. not, no; She's not going to earn points in the basketball game.
8. never, no; I never read a book to teach me how to embroider.
9. not, no; Mrs. Jenkins is not an expert at horseback riding.
10. not, no; I do not have talent in singing.

Page 25
Answers will vary.

Page 26
Answers will vary.

Page 27
Answers will vary.

Page 28
1. Aunt Carrie lives in Bethany, Missouri.
2. My dog, Marley, loves the snow in Alaska.
3. Ms. Nadir hopes to travel to Europe in July.
4. Grandpa lives on Friendly Street in Boston, Massachusetts.
5. Dear Jonathan, Thank you for the flowers you sent last Sunday.
6. Dr. Rosic isn't accepting new patients until December.
7. The girl stared at the spider, and then yelled, "A tarantula!"
8. I hope to see you soon. Sincerely, Annie.
9. We usually celebrate Easter in March or April.
10. Dad lives in the town of Oak View in California.

Page 29
Senator Jones; Monday; Los Angeles; America; August; Halloween; Uncle Rudy; New Mexico; Birch Street; Germany.

Page 30

Part I
1. Last Wednesday, Mrs. Stevens found a stray cat.
2. She examined it for an i.d. tag. It read M.B.
3. "Mr. Stevens, what should we do?" she asked her husband.
4. "Take it to Dr. Barnes at the animal hospital," he suggested.
5. Mrs. Stevens found the vet on River St. and drove over.
6. "Dr. Barnes is out today," said the receptionist. "You'll have to see Dr. McConnell."
7. Dr. McConnell examined the cat.
8. "It looks healthy, Mrs. Stevens," he said.
9. Mrs. Stevens put up fliers that said, "Cat found on West 5th Ave."
10. Mr. Bates called the next day to claim his beloved cat named "Mrs. Boots."

Part II
1. Ave.	6. Mrs.
2. St.	7. Dr.
3. Rd.	8. etc.
4. Pl.	9. i.d.
5. Mr.	10. P.O.

Page 31
1. I've always wanted to see Tucson, Arizona.
2. Finally, I left my house in Sheridan, Wyoming.
3. I started driving on June 14, 2003.
4. I ended up in Tucson on June 19, 2003.
5. "Dear Mom," I wrote. "I love the desert."
6. I'm driving up to Phoenix, Arizona, tomorrow.
7. Wish you were here. Love, Sally"
8. I met a woman from Ventura, California.
9. We have the same birthday: October 24, 1980."

Page 32
1. My Aunt Michele runs a deli in Juno, Alaska.
2. The deli is located at 21 Lincoln St.
3. Uncle Scott helps Aunt Michele run the deli.
4. They had a grand opening on July 19, 2003.
5. Dr. Robinson baked a beautiful cake for the occasion.
6. Aunt Michele wrote him a letter later, addressed to 41 12th Ave.
7. "Dear Dr, Robinson," she wrote. "Thank you for the lovely cake. My husband would like the recipe. Sincerely, Michele."
8. Now the deli serves chili, sandwiches, cake, etc., to hungry customers.

Answer Key (cont.)

Page 32 *(cont.)*

9. People come from as far away as Rome, Italy, to eat at Aunt Michele's deli.
10. Have you ever been to New York City, New York?
11. I went to a deli there on December 31, 2000.
12. Mr. Soprano owns that deli, so I wrote to him.
13. "Dear Mr. Soprano," I wrote. "Thank you for the free bagels. They are almost as good as my aunt's. Sincerely, Johnny."
14. One day, Mr. Soprano, who was on vacation, came to Aunt Michele's deli.
15. We all had a great time visiting, sharing recipes, and showing him around town.

Page 33

Part I

1. I'll; wi
2. shouldn't; o
3. we're; a
4. she's; i
5. they're; a
6. I'm; a
7. couldn't; o
8. can't; no
9. you'll; wi
10. he'll; wi
11. I'd; woul
12. he's; i
13. you're; a
14. she'd; ha

Part II

1. They'll
2. shouldn't
3. can't
4. She's
5. I'm
6. she'll
7. They're
8. We'll
9. There's
10. It's
11. We're
12. I'll
13. You'll
14. We'd
15. mustn't

Page 34

Part I

1. Jill's drum set
2. John's photos
3. Aunt Lisa's canary
4. Mom's car
5. friend's gift
6. teacher's desk
7. Cathy's dictionary
8. Mike's foot
9. Grandma's dishes
10. classroom's film projector
11. Father's mug
12. Grandpa's cat
13. state's money
14. house's yard
15. airplane's passengers

Part II

1. I borrowed Uncle Tony's shovel.
2. I needed it to work in Mother's garden.

3. The dirt's consistency was rocky.
4. I put on my aunt's gloves.
5. I wore my mother's floppy hat.
6. The sun's heat beat down on me.
7. I planted my sister's tomato seedlings.
8. California's weather is good for growing tomatoes.
9. My mother's tomatoes looked healthy.
10. Suddenly, the shovel was in my dog's mouth.
11. The scarecrow's face looked amused.
12. My uncle's face looked angry.
13. I bought him a new shovel from our town's hardware store.
14. I also bought the store's best dog leash.
15. My dog's howls woke up the earthworms when I put him on his new leash.

Page 35

1. contraction; possessive
2. possessive; contraction
3. contraction; possessive
4. possessive; contraction
5. possessive; contraction
6. contraction; possessive
7. contraction; possessive
8. possessive; contraction
9. contraction; possessive
10. possessive; contraction

Page 36

1. "When will you be home?" Louise asked her mother.
2. Mom thought a moment, then replied, "Very soon."
3. "Can you pick up some milk," Louise said, "if you're stopping at the store?"
4. "Sure," Mom said. "I'll buy eggs, too."
5. "Thank you," replied Louise.
6. Mom hung up, then called back. "I love you," she said.
7. "I love you, too," Louise answered.
8. "Drive safely," she added.
9. Mom laughed. "Of course," she said.
10. Louise ended the call by saying, "Goodbye."

Page 37

1. Bill woke up at 6:30 this morning.
2. He hoped to make the 7:10 bus.
3. At 7:00, he spilled coffee on his white shirt.
4. At 7:10, his dog brought a muddy bone into the house.
5. Bill put the dog in the bathtub at 7:20.
6. He missed the bus at 8:10.
7. Bill didn't get to work until 9:14.
8. "Work starts at 8:30!" his boss yelled.
9. "I woke up at 6:30," Bill stammered.
10. His boss cried, "Next time, wake up at 5:30!"

Pages 38–39

Answers will vary.

Pages 40–45

1. B	12. C	23. A	34. A
2. D	13. D	24. C	35. B
3. A	14. A	25. B	36. C
4. C	15. C	26. A	37. D
5. D	16. B	27. D	38. A
6. A	17. C	28. B	39. B
7. C	18. D	29. D	40. C
8. D	19. C	30. C	41. C
9. B	20. A	31. B	42. D
10. A	21. D	32. D	
11. C	22. A	33. C	